Taking My Breath

Cassandra was born and raised in the Hunter Valley region of NSW where she lives with her husband, John. She completed a PhD in English Literature at the University of Newcastle, Australia, and is currently a Conjoint Fellow there in the School of Humanities and Social Science. The focus of her thesis is Ecocritical Theory and Ecopoetics. Her work appears in various anthologies such as *A Slow Combusting Hymn*, and in journals such as *The Australasian Journal of Ecocriticism and Cultural Ecology*, *Plumwood Mountain*, *Antipodes* (USA), *Southerly*, *Meanjin*, *Overland*, *Mascara Literary Review*, *Eureka Street* and *Earthlines* (UK).

Cassandra J. O'Loughlin

Taking My Breath

Ecopoems

Acknowledgements

Grateful acknowledgement is made to the editors of the following journals in which many of these poems first appeared: *Antipodes* (USA), *Meanjin*, *Mascara Literary Review*, *Overland*, *EarthLines* (UK), *Cake* (UK), *Eureka Street* and *Southerly*.

The poem 'Floods' was first published in *From the Earth to the Table* by Catchfire Press, Dangar, NSW, 2008. Special thanks to the editors Katharine Aitken et al.

The poems 'Floods' and 'Touch and Flow' were subsequently published in *A Slow Combusting Hymn: Poetry from and about Newcastle and the Hunter Region*, ASM (Association of Stories in Macau), Macao, published in association with Cerberus Press, Markwell, NSW, 2014. Special thanks to the editors Kit Kelen and Jean Kent.

The poem 'A Spot in Time' was published in *Beneath the Valley*, Catchfire Press, Dangar, NSW, 2005. This poem won the Catchfire Press Poetry Prize in 2004. Special thanks to the editors.

I would like to express my sincere appreciation to Kim Cheng Boey, Judith Beveridge, Christopher Polnitz and my husband John for their encouragement.

I acknowledge the traditional custodians of the lands about which I write, and pay respect to the Elders past, present and future.

Taking My Breath: Ecopoems
ISBN 978 1 76041 499 3
Copyright © text Cassandra J. O'Loughlin 2018
Cover design by Cassandra L. Kayser using a photograph taken by Cassandra J. O'Loughlin on the Hawkesbury River, NSW

First published 2018 by
GINNINDERRA PRESS
PO Box 3461 Port Adelaide 5015 Australia
www.ginninderrapress.com.au

Contents

Driving Inland	9
Touch and Flow	18
Floods	23
South of Birubi on Newcastle Bight	25
Belonging	28
Muloobinbah	30
Yesterday	32
Rhythm and Dance	33
A Spot in Time	35
The Coalminer	37
Nourishment	38
Encounters	39
Picture Postcards	44
The Red Chair	46
The Rainbow Lorikeet	47
The Room and the Tree	48
The Utterances of a Child	50
Luminescence	51
Enduring Things	52
River Guide	54
To Paint the Day	56
The Bogong Moth	57
Tending Our Lives	58
Sea Change	59
On the Flight of a Daughter	63
Where the wilful weather-life wanders	64
Homespun	66
Notes	67

For my husband, John

'Only as we begin to notice and to experience, once again, our immersion in the invisible air do we start to recall what it is to be fully a part of this world... As the regime of self-reference begins to break down, as we awaken to the air, and to the multiplicitous Others that are implicated, with us, in its generative depths, the shapes around us seem to awaken, to come alive...'

– David Abram, *The Spell of the Sensuous* (260)

'Ecopoetry' is a relatively new term for describing contemporary poetry that has a strong ecological emphasis and an ecocentric perspective. It moves beyond the scope of 'landscape' and 'nature' poetry. While precise definitions vary, ecopoetry implies responsibility for the environment. It is concerned with preserving the stability and integrity of the natural world. Ecopoetry is a positive affirmation of our embeddedness in ecological relationships.

Driving Inland

'…Winning does not tempt that man.
This is how he grows: by being defeated, decisively,
by constantly greater beings.'
– Rainer Maria Rilke, 'The Man Watching'

i Beyond the Blue Mountains of New South Wales

It was when I said,
Success isn't about winning,
it's enduring to the end
in all your vulnerability,
that the outrageous continent of sky
seemed to arch and pummel the bony escarpment
now trembling in the rear mirror.

He…he said,
Success, like truth, is as a mountain;
you'd roam its ridges and gullies a long time
with your thoughts trading in the elements
and not notice it changing as it changes you.
Then he appeared
in the primal soundness of undug soil.
In the heat of that day
the road over the old-penny-like plain spilled
over the horizon's squat copper lip.

It was when I quoted the poet:
*If we surrender to earth's intelligence
we could rise up rooted, like trees*
that we stood together, alone,
as if dust particles rising, drifting,
fragile souls hitting the atmosphere
with bursts of light.

When he said,
*Truth is the colour of homesickness,
the sleep of a baby, the breath of a fox;
it is the briny tide of your stunned arrival
at no language*
I no longer needed the map.
The distance is immaterial and longest,
the day irrelevant, the smell of summer strongest,
all-consuming and otherworldly.

How far must we go
before all that fashions us is clear?
Not just derived from parentage,
but also from the elements.
I wonder the percentage of water
in an adult body. How long would I last
in the wind and the heat? How long
the ants, the lone hawk circling?

How much must we take on faith
every second of our lives
in order not to float off the planet?
To have faith is to walk to the edge of the light,
then step out into the darkness.

It seems we're following a trail
to the rim of the earth.
'Hell's Gate' hinged on hardwood flashes past.
Three far-off trees planted decades back
in a straight-veranda-line
merge in sluggish choreography
as my daughter's voice crackles from the coast
and fills the small world of our car.
Where are you? she asked, as if it matters.
I don't know exactly, I said,
*somewhere between Hay and Balranald,
the only marker a hawk combing the blue sky.*

Earlier, as if to sign a certain spot:
two men planting fence-posts,
an emu following close behind
scratching its name in the loosened earth.

The grubby sheep wake to the same tough grasses –
all nature growing loose for the want of rain.

The road, a waking lizard, is teaching us
the meaning of dust. It keeps coaxing us
into this land's legends of defeat and betrayal
although, strangely, it encourages belief
in hills to climb, and the oceans
yet to spill tides into our late years.
Like a moth flustering at a lamp
I am awake to the palpable whiff of dying,
circling the plains with the stars
in their colossal demise,
the willy-willies and curlicues
quickening my pulse, taking my breath.

ii The Hay Plains

That night it seemed all the voices of family
crossed over to the other side
were circling back, on short-lived visits
so far from home, the ore of yearning in them,
posting the scent of linen, rosemary, and camphor chests,
their breath across these sparse grasslands
warm and pungent as loam, each one
a phrase remembered,
a backward glance at mishaps
and miracles,
some voices lost in the candid dust
that settles in the delicate cancelli of our bones.

Nan and Min had never travelled
this far in their long lives.
Sensing the voices of the dead
whispering as I squatted
by the shallow roadside swale
the night's flash storm had filled with hail, I said,
Sit down with me, watch the frozen rain thaw
and sink into the thirsty, red earth.
I kept my mind clear as the ice, trusted the feel
of what treasures my thoughts have known.
I reached to touch Nan's hand.
There was a sigh
that released her long white hair from its pins.
It fell to her shoulders in the budding light.
Min handed her a bowl of fresh rainwater
to wash her hair. Afterwards
she used it to drench the cabbages. Sure enough,
when the hail had melted
they were gone
back to the rich, dark soil of their coastal valley home.

My mother often comes from beyond the veil,
toting some creature or another she has rescued.
I see her now sitting on a log, a spaniel on her lap.
At her side, a damaged magpie
that healed well, but often runs to the gate
and barks when visitors come.
I don't think the bird's identity was lost
but rather, like my mother,
it is exploring a new way of being.

So now I pause for the wild thing to come
trailing its footprints in my threadbare youth,
ousting something old and oppressive burning there.
I wait for the taste of the fulfilling song,
the impeccable binding of lost souls
to every restless thing.

iii The Outback

I can't remember if it was outside
one of those blink-and-miss, spaced-out towns
from yesterday:
Weethalle, Goolgowi or Gunbar

we saw the exhausted seed heads
heaped up to the canopy of the roadside trees;
a long flaxen cloud we tunnelled through,
opening to bright glimpses of stubbled fields.

Curly windmill grass
blown from the company of coolabah, mulga, ironwood?
Perfectly spherical: fifteen spikes, each a hand-span,
rigid, spreading from the tip of the stalk

in different planes to catch whatever wind
that navigates back and forth the wide terrain,
the seeds freed perhaps in the Wimmera
or at a mid-western margin of a claypan.

The one I placed on the back seat to study
seems to be growing more and more like me:
fragile, restless, almost to the end of the road,
our offspring scattered to the four winds.

iv On the Russet Claypan

We could go back to the earth
here on the russet claypan,
rest side by side in the ground nest of a bird,
buried under a tent of feathers and bones,
the two of us, peering between the bird's lanky legs
at the mare's tails in the washed-out-cotton sky,
at the ruddle-coloured sheep ruffled in the wind,
like the plains wanderers, dodging cloven hooves,
our deeper lives going from strength to strength.

Amid the bright stars' indigo blanket
I found in a dream my image
thatched out of spinifex and artesian spillage,
as though coming to pass
as everything comes to pass.

v The Murray-Darling Basin

Alone at the confluence of two great rivers:
the Murray and the Darling.
The sky gathers low.
The waters marry and grow more secretive,
rushing unnoticed, indifferent to banks and borders,
finding the best way, summoning birds
that fly wary, abandoned, yet content
to neither sow, nor reap, nor gather into barns.

I knock at the door of the secrets in me.
I am on a raft cut loose in quick currents,
defeated by constantly greater beings,
praying in the hush between
the bending of light and the thunder's clap,
but from my lips glisten the bubbles of my breathing,
those droplets of persisting faith.

The rain is bucketing down.
I miss my mother.
The tiny dash between birth and death
is all we have on this earth.
Where do I go from here?

vi   The Mallee Highway

Another day and the car speeds on.
The GPS hasn't spoken for hours.

The sun is again planted in the sky's clear paddock,
this time off the Murray at Renmark.

It strobes our rear-vision through a wash of aureolin
that bleeds into a pale rose-madder at the grass line.

The rough-bitten Mallee exhales the dust
as we lick the speed limit.

The seed head on the back seat is holding its breath,
waiting for the wind to change.

A hundred years from now
no one will know.

vii   The Adelaide Hills

Now, I stand here
in light coming at a grazing angle
lost in the moment,
arms loaded with warm bread
from the little bakery.
Like a warm handshake the earth grips
my soles as if a meeting is taking place.
I must have looked a long time
over the small houses and the fields,
and at the seed head that has come so far
now giving itself to a sudden breeze
when I opened the car door,
drifting higher and higher
over the gentle hills,
proven fresh on its own terms,
valid as my own small animal cry.

Touch and Flow

i

Their tail feathers flicked fan-like
as though being held in the hands of ladies,
the apostlebirds, or the Happy Family
as country people prefer.

They ran and strutted around
the paperbark tree near the back door
and ascended the branches
in quaint leaps, issuing a grating cry

when I stepped out onto the flagstone porch
and leaned against the wall to pull wellies on; there
where Anne had seen a brown snake
against the warm bricks last spring.

We pressed a vee in the fence's middle string
and stumbled across the verdant ground
that was spongy after the heavy rains:
cattle-cropped, open land.

The creek pulsed over pebbles and taupe sand
to the pooled heart of the acreage
where, in the flood of '99, Sasha,
the Setter, 'as gentle as a lamb,'

was garrotted on barbed wire
swinging loose as a necklace.
The water lapped up and over the mown lawn
to where the old church pew sat in the shade

of the paperbark tree Anne planted
when she first came to Moonan Flat.
Yes, the tree near the back door
where I saw the apostlebirds – twelve of them,

at least.

ii

It was in the foothills, an hour's walk
from the house, the brief August light bleeding
through the wind-stripped and stilled canopy

brightening on her, when she whispered, *Listen.
Listen to this*. When I put my ear to the tree,
there was something pulsing.

Now, since she is not here, I search for it
everywhere. I heard it in a night fog on Italia Road
when the gate was opened over the cattle ramp

and the veranda light, way off,
was dimly haloed. It could have been
a bicycle chain, hesitating, starting again, one note,

two. Near, yet remote.
And again at the end of another
long walk where there was a hearth

that had lost its home,
the brick chimney probing an empty sky,
the people moved on, then dead, and missed.

Each time sounding more urgent, but then
silent for weeks. Not seeing it does not matter,
the sound is enough. Just knowing it is still there,

the song that family is.

iii

My twig-snapping, leaf-rustling arriving
on the mountain is not the same
as experiencing the wild place. The
lichen-covered, seepage-of-decay sort of wildness.

And the stillness. When you appear
as though you have grown out of the earth,
life begins again its journey
into the next moment. And the next.

Knowing there is a breath-held fear of you
is the worst and the best of it. Fear separates
and unites. You come to know
life and death fit you precisely.

Then the ardent wattlebird rides
his aerial boundary, takes you in, as do the leaves
grown in cellular density across the sky's flutter,
and words turn green on your tongue's litmus.

The brush turkey with his bright yellow cravat,
businesslike in his urgent attention
to detail, scratching and reshaping
his world, ignores you. Your sameness

and difference are clear. Up here
it is possible to distinguish between
alone and lonely. Missing someone so much
you talk to the trees.

iv

Have you noticed how we see the eucalypts in their auburn-
tipped newness but not again until they are old, and how
the land is not detached but engrossed with renewal? The way
time plays with your thoughts and you are lost in those dull

sclerophyll hills since Anne is gone. The ghost gums seem to traipse
about like Virgil's shades, and it is as if you are a soul transfixed
in a dusky coracle, or roaming under the veneer of your life,
finding the human heart is a pool for suffering. You are as fragile

as the ground orchid, balanced on a threadlike stem, nourished
by the fall and decay. Do you wonder if God is tough and green?
And have you ever felt, when the darkness is coming on
and you are nearing home, as though the wattle at the veranda

seems to light something in you, or how the smell of clematis
turns your mind to spring, to the jasmine arched over the gate's
squeak and click, to the bees? Oh, the bees' wonderful keenness
for detail, trafficking beyond the notion of boundaries, quietly

communicative as today's willy-nilly wind at the creek.
A feeling, lithe as the swallows over the pond's opalescence,
you struggle to fasten down: that no poem can paint the soft-
stepping, seed-palmed sunrise, or the shock of coiled flesh.

Sometimes I find inklings tucked away in my mind, tangled
as wrens' nests, yet communal and solid as the apostlebirds'
wattle and daub: about composition, the country light,
the wild, wordless language, the colour – unpredictable,

as in the flow of wetted pigments on watercolour paper, and flowing
through the hearts of dark stars who drifted light as smoke
over the ruminant earth, over the hearth that was carried away
on the dingo's howl at dawn, and over the long silence after.

Floods

They sway their hips
like suede-dressed courtesans

these late herded cows from the flash-flooded fields
and a dairy awash bail-high

from the levy spill at Oakhampton;
their orphaned udders and blood-plum eyes

catch my headlight's glare.
Their names are springing from the grassy fields

of my childhood.
Strawberry, Petunia, Bella, Donna…

They're dancing with a tired blue dog, and a man
who's relearning the rain and the narrow terrain.

Remembering, I peel back the tar and the aggregate, expose
a stubbled hillside scored by cart and buggy furrows,

go back to other floods
that have poulticed this earth's ailing chest,

and back to Eliza from Sussex,
who sailed on a little piece of England

to work the Hunter's alluvial soil in days sunny
as peeled corn; to the unknown grasses days,

when the children came running to the milk jug
like poddies to a rattled bucket.

She gathered the remnants of her clan
around the starched white cloth of discipline,

untangled their cantankerous colonial knots,
and nudged them as the wood duck does

out of her home in the gum trees.
They learnt to swim for dear life.

And to a raft of women who voyaged down
the changing family names

from Eliza to my mother,
women who strode into their season

of ripening, faithful
to the ebb and flow of their destinies.

I belong to this tribe
whose children wore thick, creamy moustaches,

who with one or two raps of their knuckles
could tell when a melon is ripe.

South of Birubi on Newcastle Bight

An evening breeze cools the hot sand
down by the shacks in Tin City
where a woman squats, scaling fish.
The iridescent scales are adding lustre
to her freckled, weathered skin.
The air smells of summer, salt.
The sea-spray is seasoning my tan,
and everything is tinged with fish-oil yellow
from the kerosene lamp and the crackling campfire.

Her grandfather built this shack
in the Depression.
It's mullet-coloured, makeshift,
with a low-hipped lean-to
that drains rainwater into a fluted tank.
Potted gardens and pumpkins
stand as if in a dole-queue,
bleached and sun-hardened.
Beachwear pegged to a rope, is wind-filled
and ghost-dancing in the dunes' creeping shadows.

All around are the vast and shifting sands,
arrested in the west by the Old Man
Banksia trees, bracken fern, mat rush and burrawang.
Small shrubs on the occasional knolls
look like old men dancing.

I tell the woman my grandfather is dead,
and I'm looking for his mate.
He's dead too, she says. *All the old ones are dead.*
A mug of tea, offered at arm's length, draws
a line in the sand between us.

She wipes the beautiful sequins from the worn blade,
as the ocean spills its long syllable
between the land and silence.
Then she scoops the prawns
from a bucket of brine
and drops them into the boiling pot.
They turn from slime green to salmon pink,
and I think:
nothing ever is as it seems.

The sun is shining
through the warp and weft of black velvet,
and a lifetime
is creeping up behind me
as if on stilts.
In the shadow of my hat
I watch the waves
rising as if behind glass,
suspending shoals of fish –
silver, catching the light.

I stride over the low-tide rooms,
periwinkle bathtubs, basins
and slap-stuck seaweed curtains.
My name is uttered
amid the litterinids: conniwinks and noddiwinks,
as if I existed in the gaps of memory
with the ghosts of the wind and the water.
There's an ancient, liquid language
over the dunes, the middens,
and a sudden, eerie chill lifts me up,
and like a great wave in the throes of being itself,
tosses me as if I were weed.

Belonging

Women, squatting on spinifex,
weave green reed baskets for the tourists.
Their skirts are a brilliant blaze
against the red earth.
Their eyes and teeth, a shock of whiteness.
Their talk, on and on,
is as old as the sand.

A wizened Elder tells stories
about the waterholes, the rocks,
the stars in their flight across the seasons.
About the Dreamtime,
Uluru, the Snake-people,
how terrible things happen
if ancient laws are violated.
Her voice is eerie
as if from deep in the earth,
resonating like the long vowels
of a didgeridoo.

Another woman, feeling movement
in the spinifex beneath her,
springs to her feet.
Cheeky blighter, she says,
and with sleight of hand
flings a snake into the air –
a Brown, writhing – its flat head
flaring against the cobalt sky.
Now their laughter
swims through the coolabah trees,
fingers the reeds
like a cool breeze.

A hawk is hovering high up,
far away. Too far away like me
belonging in that way
to this curious land.

Although, on this maestro of a day
that holds the earth up to the sun as if in invocation,
it is clear we are each as siblings,
our river of being sometimes gentle and deep,
at other times quick and powerful
and rushing towards the waiting soil.

Muloobinbah

Before I knew it Newcastle's Crown Plaza had crept
over Merewether Street Wharf like a lizard,
it's legs planted deep in the Hunter's mud. It's ragged
neck a promenade over the water: concrete on petrified
timbers where I sit thinking.

The line of my thoughts is snagged here, on the rocks
        of '62: diesel and sea-smells;
        a weathered shed; a tethered ship –
        black and red. The vessel will sink
        to its plimsoll line under the weight
        of cargo from the industries, and slide out
        on the rising tide of Asia.

The shadows of sailing ships are carved into this new concrete
as if the sun rising over the Pacific is still pointing landward.
    This is the place
        is written in the salty wind.
In the grip of a southerly buster, the ghosts
of the old mariners
are wailing for England and Ireland.

And others   dark stars   are lamenting
    the change of Muloobinbah
    losses
            of the Woromi
    people of the ferns mangroves paperbarks.

My heart searches the silence				outside
its own story. Do we all not hope
for our children to dance as moths			around
			the warm light of family,

in a place we call home?
Home is not only a miamia or a house,
an address where someone			waits
for news of a loved one, but a
			time-
					layered place
						where generations
							walk
			and turn to
				dust
feeding spirit earth.

Place owns the rainbow between white   and   black
memories stacked in the self's archives.
The lizard squats
			on our sad, chequered histories

and I sit hitting a stick on an old pylon. The gulls might see
the last Stockton-bound ferry		leaving the pier,
but by then I will probably be			gone.

Yesterday

A storm roiled in an icy blue-green front
and set the early light back an hour.
The willie wagtail, in his surplice and cassock,
retraced his steps to stillness, and the giddy wrens,
Blues with their Jennies, vanished.

After the bucketing, the earth squeezed
its citrus everywhere, the trees scintillated
a trillion suns. The dam receded under the sheen,
and the scent of pollens punctuated the silence.
I rested easy in my age. The wrens returned,

thirty or so, like wind-blown flowers on the lawn
and along the long, low sills, their rivals danced
in the glass, the pane thin between us.
Then, I vowed never to worry again
about this vertiginous life.

But, the dazzle dissolved too soon,
and things were as they had been earlier,
except the dam had filled, and become darker.
Old-age stepped from the stony rim,
with her palms extended,

and yesterday now blooms with a new flourish.

Rhythm and Dance

i.m. Lily May Sutton Haynes (1889–1970)

i

As a child I asked, *Do angels really come?*
only to hear Nan say, *They come to attend you
when your time's over*, only to hear my mother say,
Brush your teeth and go to bed.

Thoughts were gathering when Nan came.
For a moment they rested on her curious expression.
I looked in vain for the sky's shining steps, the last amen,
the wind's gathering of every finished thing.

Calm to calm, we spoke our names
and soft flames of fondness flickered between us.
I found myself altered, growing buoyant
by her nearness. She smiled, clasped her small hands,

and was gone.

ii

Thumbing through windfalls and timeworn papers
that are like antique wallpaper cracking at a touch
and showered with moulds full-blown as roses
among the branches and roots of our family,

I find her coming to me in copperplate recipes,
in the rhythm of eggs breaking on the rim,
as if she's conducting a symphony
while many suns are setting in her bowl.

Step forward, Nan, I say, *once more for me*
perform your thread and shuttle doily dance,
tatting knots and picots around a bed of jonquils,
accept from my garden this sprig of rosemary.

iii

She walks out of an icy morning into the cold
kitchen, the door letting the winds come in,
the scuttle filled with coal wet from the frost,
her fingers inflamed, frost-bitten, coal-dusted.

There is the distant clamour of shunting locos,
skips clunking on sleepers, small birds like keys
turning quietly in the casuarinas, but always
the smell of coal gas in winter's dark declension.

Nan, I call out, *reach for your full potential*
on the other side of the veil. I'm thinking
of the Illawarra Flame in our summer garden.
I imagine you blossoming like that.

A Spot in Time

I was on my grandmother's lawn
in a mining town,
a labyrinth of tunnels miles below.
The air was hot, and heavy
with the smell of coal gas
and dew damp grass.
A still, moonless summer night,
streetlights winking, far off.

Arms spread, I twirled
round and round on the spot,
spinning with the stars,
repeating, *I'm seven today, I'm seven today*.
My fingers dug into the grass
like a garden fork when I fell.
A force from within the earth
held me a moment.
Wonder opened my mouth.
Then, my body as if floating: a stray star
drifting into folds and folds
of dark space.

At that moment
I realised I was in essence me,
Cassandra,
separate, unknown and unknowable
as the sparrow or the ant.

My mother stood over me,
her head in the stars.
My little sister tumbled beside me,
scatty, giggly, somehow changed.

Time begins, when you know
with eyes closed you're visible,
and when the nervous bird announces
your nearness.

The Coalminer

i.m. Edgar Haynes (1911–1963)

Because he rode a dim shaft of light back through the ages,
I want to ask him about the locksmiths in the Permian rooms
of fossilised sunlight where the tunnels travel through
the glossopteris forests to Richmond Vale, about the flames
and the end of his dreams, and about coal wagons like boats.

Above, light is rocked at dawn in the cradles of creek beds
where I have seen myself mapping the coalfields, and counting
the cows and cornflowers that hike the tracts to the hillside
left ajar for him, where the wattle lights candles at the gate
and the fairy wrens nestle their young in webby dewdrops.

His death was troubling as a snake-slough on a doorstep.
I heard in July's frosty air, the sleepers groaning as the wagons
flashed in a row, as if his remains were its payload when
the last train heaved out of Stanford Merthyr. Forests hard
as stone keep coming with puffs of smoke and a cargo of ashes.

Nourishment

The elderly man and woman travelling opposite me on the Indian Pacific train are close and similar, as two halves of the one walnut. He wears a soft flat cap. Her head is wound with long, blue-grey plaits. Their clothes are like those worn by the refugees of the fifties: dowdy, but neat and practical. He's reading *The Australian*. The pages are spread across both their laps, but she doesn't mind. They haven't spoken, hardly exchanged a glance. She watches the changing but unchanging landscape. He sits near the aisle, and occasionally leaves his seat, folding the newspaper where he's left off reading. After a while, and seemingly in keeping with some inviolable arrangement, she erects a small bench over their knees, pulling, as if from a secret compartment, a white cloth with two matching napkins, a small serrated knife, two plates, crusty rolls, cold cuts, capers, capsicum, olives, sauerkraut and pungent cheeses. One cheese is a thick, rounded wedge with brown, cloth-scored skin; another is white and blue-veined. I wait for a bottle of wine. I'm astonished by their uncompromising sense of self-preservation. They've done this before, perhaps intending never to go hungry again. They eat with the passion of Latin lovers. The land tumbles recklessly by – the red desert, dry river-beds, sparse mulga and tussock grass – filling the gap between them and their delicatessen.

Encounters

The clouds had emptied their buckets for days, up and down the coast, over towns and small holdings and virgin highlands, so now the stillness over the fields seems novel, as if the intense weather low was what we needed to begin afresh, in the sound of stillness, its mayhem of small biological awakenings, the wisdom I have waited to learn from all things moving around us: in Coffee's ruined shack under the jollop vine, the habits of the welcome swallow above the rafters; the platypus in the river surfacing with a muscly shine and hollow plop; the perfect circles of ripples widening, losing themselves in the water weed; a shiver in the reeds; the grasses glistening under the broken clouds.

I was standing in a rain-blistered blackberry patch when a magpie bolted from the wet bed of the paddock. The crack of a stick in the bush spooked the horses. I followed their gaze. There, a stone's throw away, a shadow of the pictures the press had painted, was the fugitive, stumbling, half-naked, bruised, and bloodied: the escapee from Long Bay prison, coming towards me, a skinny fourteen-year-old kid in shorts and sandshoes. In his exhaustion, it seemed the blow from a deep breath could topple him.

Almost by instinct I stepped forward. Startled, he became a chameleon, and then a swamp mahogany. His skin was barked, and his dark hair unkempt, wiry as bottlebrush. His breath was coming short. He lurched forward, sculling the air like a turtle out of water, waving the ambush quiet aside. He smelled of neep tide in an estuary. His words came as if a torrent cornered in a ravine. The aquifer of my memory has tampered with the forensics in the long years since:

> *A long time I ran over the Chase prodding myself*
> *into narrow ravines, toppling over gravelly gorges,*
>
> *up to my neck in mangroves and quicksand, in rain*
> *and hail and heat, the grebe's sodden alarum*
>
> *stirring up bullets to assault and pepper the last resort*
> *where I'd been morsing the distance between us.*

I lifted the locks of the jollop and pushed him beneath the shack's crossbeams. I sat on the boards beside his slumped form and perked my ears, naïve as a wallaby.

> *In this dream I am walking alone in a fairground:*
> *the storm that pelts rocks at my head*
>
> *scatters the crowds; pigs with deceitful grins*
> *are at the stalls of fortune-tellers and tattooists.*
>
> *When I front one to ask directions he bites*
> *off my tongue.*

His words beat a path to my ears, trampled the long grass of my youth. Here, a mile from the garden where my grandmother had put down her roots and the fowls were cooped against the fox. A butcherbird's painstaking song streamed along the gully, neoteric notes as if budding from the water in sympathy with the shades that inhabit the crags and crannies of the escarpment.

I knew him by the news bulletins that droned through my grandmother's house, drafted for drama as in a murder movie. Gran, who with gusto shouldered the blows and rolled with the punches of boxing on the radio, sitting in the dark to save power, found a new focus: having long ago joined the silent and unassembled fraternity of mothers, she followed the progress of the prodigal through the Chase to the Hawkesbury's biblical wilderness, left milk and manna on the veranda, her prayers for rain to wash all trace of him from the noses of the tracker dogs, answered. She said,

— *He must have a mother somewhere, worried sick.*

Something entered the shack in that one moment when the vine was lifted, not the runaway alone, not a gusty, rain-laden southerly, or the nameless officers armed with high-powered rifles, pistols and shot guns. Those gentle familiars who climb the steps and feature in the lambent glow on the walls of imagination are valid. They must be taken in, fed and offered a pillow.

> *Motes are swimming behind my eyelids, Cass,*
> *my head is watery, my bed adrift*
> *in a tidal swell that is pulling in the baitfish*
> *and the sharks are circling.*
>
> *Bring the oat fields of your skin to my lips, listen*
> *to the last-minute confession of a condemned man:*
> *I want to die cognizant, ideograms like 'love'*
> *and 'trust' tumbling from your fingertips.*

Across the valley, evening fleeced the trees, the creek and fields blurred again to rain. When I came back with milk and cake, smuggled out of the house after the creek-bed of Gran's mind had darkened and faded into sleep, he was still drifting in and out of the silted drains of delirium.

*I don't know what to do, mother.
Each day before the whistlers stir in the heath,
a small boy who looks like me comes up
from the beach and sits by my door.*

*For three weeks he has come carrying a nest
with two pale blue eggs, a silvereye's, I think:
cup-shaped, bound together with spider web.
He doesn't speak, just sits there at the end*

*of December holding the nest, and he leaves
before the silvereyes flood the myrtle.
He stopped coming two days ago. The nest
was left amongst the stones.*

*When I lifted the one remaining egg to the light
I found it was empty.
Mother, what have I done with my life?*

*

*My mother said you will be all right:
heaven is not far away; in the meantime
there is plenty in the pantry –
young shoots and fruits of the wombat berry,
Warrigal greens, the seed of kangaroo grass.
The flowers of the grass tree soaked in water
offer a sweet drink; use water, son,
with all its music still in it.*

On the third day he was gone. There was an absence in the shack you could feel, some tangible ghost of dialects, a spinner of words, his message to me left in the tidal rings of milk in the bottle.

A week later, when he looked for sunlight on Sugarloaf Mountain, he heard the dogs and the police closing in. The horses stood stock-still in the clearing and watched him. His pursuers followed their gaze. A shadow of the man stepped from behind a blue gum, head down, hands in the air, as if bowing to an unknown god.

Now and again the welcome swallow comes and goes with a flash of metallic blue-black and russet; I open the window of my mind and let her through. The jollop works its way between the slats of my years. Coffee's place still stands in the stilted masonry of my memory. All are wanderers bent on mouthing back his words.

At times I think what makes us the way we are is neither ancestry nor circumstance but something found between the life we dream and the one we live through our encounters, real or imagined, as we wade the stony stream of our existence. I think of the man now I have grown fifty years away and stand at last in the dead centre of a suburb in the loose-fitting shirt of a sunlit winter looking back at the receding hairline of the wilderness.

Picture Postcards

for Kim Cheng Boey

You say you are an odd pagoda
among the orthodox glories.
Always in search of an elsewhere,
you stand on the narrow peak
of a sacred mountain of the Middle Kingdom,
the one where the Ancients played chess
and talked poetry and Buddhism.
The Chess Pavilion of Mt Huashan is
Chinese calligraphy penned over clouds
that skim the deep gorges;
the uppermost handrail you grip
against sudden annihilation
is four lost and floating eyelashes
on the postcard you sent with the hope
that the new year will bring more poems.

Your postcard from the Lehling Book Shop shows
monks on the hairpin path
to the high-perched, white-daubed Rizong Monastery.
The monastery is like the clustered nests
of welcome swallows.
The silence of Ladakh after the tourist season
appeals to you, the poet,
but even the crows, sparrows and magpies
inhabiting the apricot groves in summer
find it difficult to withstand the winter chill.
Is this where you encounter the monk
who smiles as if he knows why you are with them,
shuttling like an alien craft
between the monasteries?

I sense you are somewhere
in India's Gokarna market,
learning to do the simple things – inhaling life
among the celeriac, aubergine and beans. Peace
is the nourishing stock for your meals,
the tastes and smells, the sacrament.
When I look into the solemn eyes
of the woman in the market's fruity light,
the cup of my mind is filled
with warm, spicy broth.
I am the voyeuring pilgrim.
By way of bridging the gap, I imagine
a speck of soil from that place
is embedded in the glue of the postage stamp.

It is a long way from teeming India
and from the Land of the High Passes
where you wonder
what the prayer flags are telling the wind,
to Plum Blossom at Sydney's QVB.
A long way from a life any one of us could have owned
to the ordinary vegetable one we are living
in this new, old country of evolving cultures.
Here, odd might mean unique
rather than uneven or at variance with.
Our land is one of contradictions and extremes –
too much is never enough, but here, time and space
might allow the breezes of inspiration
to tinkle the many bells of your stupas.

The Red Chair

My mansion in heaven is like this, he said from where he sits in the red armchair that was custom-made for someone who must be all of seven feet tall, and built like a barrel. It took some time and ingenuity to remove the doors and the architraves, he told me, too squeeze it like a lemon to fit. And now it's by the fire that is spitting sparks onto the aeons-old hearth braced to withstand the weather long after the white ants and fungi feasting on the piers have taken the home back to the earth.

He made this new hearth out of a slab of granite someone had thrown out thinking it old-fashioned, cutting it wide enough so the sparks from the logs that he scrounged from the housing development wouldn't burn the plush carpet he picked up after someone had grown tired of the colour.

As if a shack were all he knew, and recycled accessories, he claimed the chair like an allotment where he would work out his last days, its threads the colour of tomatoes or capsicum, or blood mingled with sweat and tears. It's not all the same to him what the sun rises on; it makes a difference dreaming in a sumptuous red chair.

While ever there are wild berries ripening into windfalls over the fence, and, even if nettles along the rocky path hitch a ride in his socks, the great giver in the sky seems to favour the bright-eyed, dribbly-jowled dog beside him in the red chair, and him too, he thinks, his thonged feet swinging a hand-span or so from the floor.

The Rainbow Lorikeet

More water than colour is what I want from a painting:
I love the bold engagement between
the pigments and the hot-pressed *papier*
but it is in the colours' vanishing edges I find the wonder.

It reminds me of the lorikeet that brought a rainbow
to our porch in December's heatwave: his muttering
at our nearness and silent acceptance of our gifts,
but my heart smiled widest at the wing-lift of his leaving.

The Room and the Tree

The autumn wind blows the magnolia tree,
shifting the shadows in the room.
In the yellow light, the grandmother
is winding wool from a skein held by the girl
who squats on the floor, looking at the photographs
and odds and ends behind glass in the whatnot.

The girl thinks the cabinet is called a whatnot
because it holds secrets about the family tree,
about the people in the old photographs
who are dead. You must whisper in this room.
Children must be seen, not heard, remembers the girl.
The ball gets bigger in the hands of the grandmother.

Hold your hands higher, says the grandmother,
who doesn't notice the man above the whatnot
winking and nodding at the girl
when the wild wind bends the tree.
A sad girl sits, as if frozen, in an imaginary room
with another whatnot and other photographs.

What's that, the girl whispers, *between those photographs?*
It's a wigwam for a goose's bridle, says the grandmother.
The girl's arms are getting tired. She hates the room,
the hovering faces, and thinks the whatnot
might as well go back to being a tree.
Why are those men dressed as soldiers? the girl

persists, but the grandmother just sighs. The girl
thinks she'll draw the people in the photographs.
Stick people sitting along the branches of a tree.
Two branches up, the grandmother
will sit, singing, swinging her legs. The whatnot
will not be in her picture, nor will the room.

I will always be inside your head, shouts the Room.
How do you say Y-P-R-E-S? The girl
spells the word, defiantly. She glares at the whatnot.
There's a cemetery cross, and a face: two photographs.
When a word's too hard, say Wheelbarrow, the grandmother
says, and the wind punches at the tree.

You're too alive for this room, whisper the photographs.
There! We're finished. Now go and play, says the grandmother.
And the girl runs off to claim her place in the tree.

The Utterances of a Child

for Claire

Surely the song larks on the Hay plains heard your call
on the land line, and the birds in the atolls of light
on the Murray. The bright-eyed quolls would have stopped
to listen in the mountain's deep-scented shade.
Certainly the koel in the fig would know it was you,
and the restless boobook that twirls curlicues in the fog.
Rain falls on my face, on my hands, as I wait for your next call.
Your voice sends out light from every syllable, every vowel
and consonant…there is no one who can explain this.
The household words gathered in your four years are sweet
raspberries at my breakfast table, wrens on my the pillow.

Luminescence

for Willow

As if naming a star for her had somehow given her wings,
at birth she glided into the room, every breath a grace-note
from the cosmos. Eyes I say, and dew, and borage blooms.
Willow Grace: the fairy wren tweet, the sugar-plum possum.

I was drawn to the eye of the moon and fell among flowers,
my poems, sparrows, glow-worms and button quails praising
the spider's spinnerets, silk, the worm's minuscule mouth,
and dewdrops glass barnacles on the wings of damselfly.

My door was opened to geese fabled to grow from the shells
of cirripedes. If I sit still they take root in my imagination
and flourish. I'm inclined to wrap fresh bread in her bib and lace
bells to her booties as defence against the will-o'-the-wisp.

I have come to hear with sharper ears the breeze and the showers
whispering the sound of her name, but also the gale's rousing notes,
the leaves' distress, the clouds' acid rain. My wings are hovering
over the nursery, or trembling in the dark, sheltering chicks.

Enduring Things

The small animal in my head at night hesitates,
then picks up the scent of an ancient route
and another place in me: the city of steel and jaded bricks,
of mills, foundries and furnaces, its locomotives grunting,
whining on tracks that sliced through the hearts
of the sweat-shiny, blackened men
whose households were regulated by the whistle
they woke or slept by.

The steelworks, like a bulker tethered
amidst chimney stacks and luffing cranes
to a bollard on the Hunter, rising out of the river mist,
silhouetted against a broad sky,
is now a thing of air in the birds' flight-path.
The coke ovens and furnaces are gone,
Platt's Channel reclaimed by waterhens, plovers,
the mangroves in the tide's ceaseless swell.

Perhaps this land wants its ancient self back:
the alluvial soil, the rocks, the wind-quarried sand
on the beach where I'm now strolling.
I think I understand how the elephant felt:
the one photographed for the *National Geographic*
as it tracked through the lobby
of the Luangwa Valley Lodge in Zambia
following an inbred path to the mango trees.

My ancient routes drift in and out of sight,
but I'm listening for familiar tribal sounds,
the South Pacific's breeze through the bush, the soft brush
of percussion and indiscriminately above that, the wind
free as the whistling kite above the foliage, above the valley.
The animal in me thrives on the insouciant life:
on the mineral hum and the taste of sunshine
at this pleasant place my solemn heart has made.

River Guide

There is something of the river in the man: in the deep-rooted, river gum country of his mind a new day floods through; stories fly from the branches of his thoughts like a flock of noisy parrots, their colours brightening as they clear the trees. He speaks otherworldly sagas of the Murray: of pubs, boutiques and brothels, kitchen gardens, jars of jam and boiled lollies; all supplied by the river on the back of sheep or timber or wheat. The village of Echuca has a conceptualised value, like the tuning fork sound of a voice vibrating out of a phonautograph, belonging to souls who walk the streets of his words, whose eyes are like the water hen's, alert to the breaking and repairing of the river's mirrors. I am left with the sensation of surfacing in the moment, as if searching for something important I must do with my life.

The man's trousers, rolled at the hem as if prepared for wading, and his shirt, are the white-grey cloud colour of the naked gums, his boots, brown-black like the bark, and chipped. At his preamble, a corella nestling in his vest says 'hello' and other words that my ears are not trained for. Hawks had robbed her of a leg and a wing. The word 'bang' is a trigger for her to play dead – her head hangs loosely over his stubby fingers. She is resurrected by a seed, sits on his collar, and then moves from one shoulder to the other around the brim of his hat: a claw and beak arrangement.

He tells us that when he was a boy he would step across the river on the bonnets of dumped cars. During the long drought years, he said, like the decade just passed. Now, beneath the river's dimples and eddies, its folds and long pleats, there is a powerful and silent undertow. Behind us, coolness swaggers and rises through the pier's tall pylons that are a forest of ancient hardwoods arranged in rigid geometry, embedded in the mud, grown green in the swirling tide that had at some distant time gouged the hill. The gums wade deep into the current. The paddle-steamer turns, churns up the muddy lair of a cod so timeworn the fishermen have not the heart to harvest it.

The morning is alive with birds: kookaburras and black cockatoos the most numerous of the raucous varieties. At each outburst, the corella cowers, finds her nest in the man's vest. Water brims the banks of the man's eyes. Words are lumped in his throat. He is quiet as a timber mill where the workers have downed tools to go home, as if he is waiting to hear the river swell, its singular and colossal muscle shifting the silt.

Back inside the car, in the lacy shade of a gnarled peppercorn tree, I curl up behind the tinted glass and weep for joy: for the covenants made and kept between the river, the trees, the man and the bird. They watch over each other, and seem to be speaking in tongues.

To Paint the Day

for Janice Naylor

She sits puddling the colours of spices and citrus
on her palate and notices a pelican coasting
like a Catalina aircraft into a tidal glimmer on the lake.

As the sun falls to its belly in the wet sand, she shifts
for a brush-sweep, loving the feel of the number nine
sable and the page strong and white as sailcloth.

Keeping the tints pure, she loads her brush,
but a boy casts his shadows over her ambition.
What are you painting? the child asks.

She leans sideways to point, but it's too late:
the sun has gone to set somewhere else.
What does it matter? she thinks. Years from now,

only she will remember the ant that walked
over an ache in her foot, the air smelling
of beached seaweed, and the pelican catching her glance

before turning with the tide on silver trevally.
And she'll walk casually into the garnishing sunset
of another day, not wanting to fix the sky to a canvas,

and not minding the child who will grow too big
for his shadow. What she feels has no brushstrokes,
and no name but sun, sand, ant, bird and child.

The Bogong Moth

Spring, and the Bogong moths coast,
yielding to northward wind currents
as if to break the natural order of things,

disrupting a rhythm, ancient and of vast significance.
This summer these dusky angels won't aestivate
draped like countless epaulettes in the cool caves

of the Snowy Mountains, their plump abdomens
no longer harvested for feasts amid trade, stories,
and dance since before linear time.

Perhaps they're pining lost moiety. Exhausted,
wings tattered, almost downless, they drift
through the city like leaves from a wintering tree.

One was lured by the light in my kitchen,
it's legs scratching the air. With fingers dancing
for a million vanished stars I put it to my lips,

and think of another kind of hunger.

Tending Our Lives

The kettle that whistled a pot of tea for the grown-ups
was cold by the time we left the timber cutter's hut, and Seili
had done sweeping the blown-in leaves from the earthen floor.

Nan and I tramped the wet track along the river's sinuous bank
brushing webby twigs and lofty invisible barriers aside,
trading our silences amid the last splitting notes of the whip-birds,

sidestepping mushrooms orchestrated in wondrous girdles of light
that glossed the tea trees, startled by the erupting commotion
of variegated voices and fluttering forms that creep and hover

through forests and anonymous grasses that have roamed
for millennia between floods and burn-offs. I learnt to fall,
to trust my heaviness, as a bird does before it can fly.

There, briefly, learning who I am, how the young sound of me
was spent in Seili's broom, and in the warmth of Nan's hands,
unaware that pathways lose all who travel them.

The hungry scrubland consumed the hut after the river ran wide
and brown over living farms and dead tree stumps. Everything
is still singing up the ponderous and miraculous incline of the earth.

The day remains a sacred place where the familial inhabit,
and in the arcane there is music, candid as the bird uttered,
eager to own us, draw us into what has slipped from our minds.

Sea Change

i.m. Gwen Harrison (1920–2009)

She was conceived in 1920 after her father returned
from the Somme, Europe's gas and dirt
still in his lungs, the colonial mother left behind.
Her life was continuous with a nation flourishing,
seasoning, sailing knot by knot
>	into the Pacific.

When I was a child she appeared to possess
a habitual temperament, impervious to alteration
– a jenny wren, darting in and out of her thicket,
red-tile-and-brick on a quarter-acre her habitat,
a pleated skirt, ice-blue twinset and pearls
>	her indelible markings.

Her family was solidified, conservative,
and complacent. She seemed content
at the centre of their universe. Yet,
in her bones there was a brewing disquiet; she knew
more than all my clumsy aspirations
>	could marshal the sense to solve.

Her children, foregrounded in this photograph,
were conscriptionists, seemingly hyphenated
between war and peace. A stiff westerly is blowing
the rose and jacaranda flowers all over
the lawn's neatness, the paths made slippery
>	by their untimely fall.

What is permanent? Not the birds or the trees.
Not the couples who rush in their transience to touch,
one or the other left wanting. Their offspring
drift into other orbits, other lifestyles.
Ingredient after ingredient, she discovered
      within what was not so much a system

but a code – vernacular, primal. It drove her
to summer north, a thousand kilometres
in a green Morris Minor with Daisy, a short-haired bitzer
and Bertha, a speckled hen. She's walking towards me, barefoot
in the sand, dressed in a mottled shift, her hair a wiry nest,
      the tank of her heart full.

*I've joined the native orchid society – Spiranthes sinensis,
ladies' tresses, Dendrobium, the 'Bardo Rose', and so on,*
she says, as she stands on one leg then the other, stork-style,
washing the sand from her feet under the tank-tap's trickle.
I comb a binocular across the tableau
      in one long blur.

Her bay home sighs and settles into the evening's
quartz glitter, open to the crickets,
the mosquitoes, the chat of the ripe-fruit bats.
The back step is worn to a dip. Heights and names
of children from another time
      are pencilled on the doorpost.

Sand percolates through the floorboards.
Bracken ferns *Pteridium esculentum* (native food
she assures me), climb the veranda steps.
Mind the hen. She's resting for her egg-a-day task.
The hen is peeping from the window of her butter-box
        in the pleasant, slow drip of her days.

Gumnuts tune the xylophone above the rafters,
the summer-dressed bunks, the ice chest,
the table, the stools, the walls, nail-holed ages ago:
tiered moorings for photographs.
Cream blossoms on the Christmas bushes
        muster russet sepals for December.

The old paper-bark is twisting and unwrapping
into pink tissue where GH loves EH is a carved wound.
A southerly buster plummets the temperature
ten degrees on the outgoing tide, the sea horses
scattered from the offshore weed plains
        ride the stirred-up ridges.

Now, a green sea swirls through the landscape of her mind.
The vegetation is nameless, neither discovered nor lost.
She's standing in the shallows of a memory,
waving a white hanky, her broad-brimmed hat blown off,
indigo veining the bay in the fading fruit salad light.
        She's smiling forever.

The bread and water of peace are on her tongue. Her sun
comes naked from the sea, goes dressed into the blue hills.
What better life for a child born of a schismatic age
than to sail knot by knot into the Pacific,
her skirt, an unfurled spinnaker billowing
        from the mast of her body.

On the Flight of a Daughter

My emotions are like split lentils in a glass bottle, the lid sealed when she dropped the house keys off 'just in-case.' Two flights to Port Douglas, cloudy weather map; a massive Low flooding Queensland's rivers. Yesterday's quake is still shaking my lentils; it shifted earth's axis, stole 100th of a second from the day. Enjoy every second I said as I waved her off, airbrushing a smile. Enjoy the Daintree; rain in rainforests makes sense. It doesn't matter if it rains when you're snorkelling on the reef: you're wet anyway. Wait and watch. There are always whorls in the sea to mark the joy the coral feels as it searches for the future. Remember it. Write it down while it's fresh. Pass it on. Three days since the Faith No More concert. Are her ears still ringing? I forgot to ask. Ten minutes to flight-time. Too late, her mobile's off. The early sun is dropping vertical bars on my desk, across the pencils, sharp, lined up. Once a fleshy pod, now the vessel is shrivelled that bore the baby.

Where the wilful weather-life wanders

If you want to farm the land you must watch for ruinous weather and understand the power of a flood. You see the clouds as cattle corralled against the gates of the mountain, jostling over the hillocks and boggy flats. Listen for the thin cry of small bent-winged birds. Smell the thickening rain. Feel in your frame a dark trembling. The seeping up from the subsoil meets the stubborn teeming from above, and together they climb the sagging fences and the orchard's quivery grasses, drown the clover pocked with Paterson's curse. It hounds the ticks, black snakes, and brown. The flood sinks its teeth into the deep roots of the peppercorn tree caught slumbering against the shed.

Clearly vigilant, the night keeps its lamp filled, its wick dry. Behind the high timber fence, the mousy-brown, sooty-faced cows take on a lively amphibiousness amongst the smells of waterweed and dungy grasses, their udders full and aching. The doors of the dairy bolt open and bang shut. The chug-a-chug of the milking machines seems to have something to do with the dairy drifting sideways into the river. As if listening for the riverbanks to break, the trees stand still, skewered with rain, and silent.

The farmer has to think about filling the kitty. The poddy calves that were suckling at fingers plunged knuckle-deep in milk, are now bundled into trucks bound for auction; a mother's anguish fades into the pot-holed distance. The auctioneer chants frantically, *Two dollar bid, now three, will ya' give me three? Going once, going twice*; the ring man is working up to the gavel's thud. *Sold!*

Now the stagnant level of morning is broken. Weather-life

rises swiftly as if from her workbench, and dances, drunker and drunker. Her presence all at once seems extraordinary. Arms wide, she breathes in with excitement the fusty air. The floods rightful claim is vindicated. The low earth feels on its skin fresh earth from the high country. We are at the edge, saying things: a flood is towards knowing.

From a safe distance, you imagine it at work on the farm: heaving the troughs, pigs and buildings in the dark; twirling the piano and doilies and dolls in whirlpools, and the marmalade just bottled this summer. Air is hauled from rooms, breathless and shouting from remoter and remoter fields. You see houses unravelling and piling like kindling against the bridge, roofs like upturned boats, and a woman, at full term, dangling puppet-like from a railing. Children are bundled without hat or boots into army ducks. Bloated cows float past. And it continues, it doesn't let up for days: its strength is astonishing.

So precise discernment might be made: open fields and a cold river deluged into – a brilliant current, unchecked and resented; wherever wilful weather-life wanders and takes forage, there is an old truth due for a next-time-around. In the meantime, when you sow your clover you must be ready with your scythe. And, rather than risk flooding the market, plant yourself in the vegetable patch and start eating.

Homespun

When I feel small in the forest,
naïve in the company of bees,
nascent alongside the sand,

when my Gaelic roots stop shy
of this antipodean rock,
I dream into being

a frame to hang my name on,
the far sound of it,
from Homer's *Iliad*, for instance,

but homespun seems truer –
Cassandra, I say, and *seeds*,
and sparrows blossom in the weeds.

Notes

'Driving Inland': Rainer Maria Rilke's poem 'The Man Watching' is found in *News of the Universe: Poems of Twofold Consciousness*, chosen, introduced and translated by Robert Bly (San Francisco: Sierra Club Books, 1995), p. 121. For the structure and dialogue, part i owes a debt to Wallace Stevens's poem 'On the Road Home' in *The Collected Poems of Wallace Stevens* (Alexandria VA: Chadwyck-Healey, Inc. *Database of Twentieth-Century American Poetry*, 1998) pp. 204–5. The words 'If we surrendered / to earth's intelligence / we could rise up rooted, like trees' in part i are from Rainer Maria Rilke's poem 'Wenn etwas mir vom Fenster fällt' in *Book of Hours: Love Poems to God*, translated by Anita Barrows and Joanna Macy (New York: Riverhead Books, 1996), p. 116. The words 'How much must we take on faith / in order not to float off the planet' in part i are adapted from first the line in part iv of Tomas Tranströmer's poem 'Schubertiana' in *News of the Universe: Poems of Twofold Consciousness*, p. 203.

'Touch and Flow': part iv was inspired by Mark Tredinnick's poem 'Have You Seen?' in *Fire Diary* (Sydney: Puncher and Wattman, 2014), p. 91.

'Rhythm and Dance': the last two lines of this poem were adapted from Michael Longley's poem 'Leaves' in *Collected Poems* (London: Jonathan Cape, 2006), p. 324.

'Encounters': this poem is about an imaginary encounter with Kevin John Simmonds, who escaped from Long Bay Prison, 9 October 1959. He was captured five weeks later in the forest near my grandmother's house at Stanford Merthyr, NSW. Gollan, Anne. 'Kevin John Simmonds (1935–1966)', *Australian Dictionary of Biography*, National Centre of Biography. Australian National University, http://adb.anu.edu.au/biography/simmonds-kevin-john-11690

'Picture Postcards': this poem refers to Kim Cheng Boey's poem 'Plumb Blossom or Quong Tart at the QVB' in *After the Fire* (Singapore: First Fruits, 2006), pp. 32–35. The reference to 'an odd pagoda / among these orthodox glories' and 'shuttling / like an alien craft' is found in Boey's poem 'Coda' in *After the Fire*, p. 154.

'The Room and the Tree': this poem was inspired by Elizabeth Bishop's poem 'Sestina' in *The Complete Poems 1927–1979* (New York: Farrar, Straus and Giroux, 1983), p. 123.

'River Guide': the phrase 'speaking in tongues' in the last line of this poem owes a debt to Michael Longley's 'The Lapwing' in *Collected Poems* (London: Cape Poetry, Random House, 2006), p. 243. It can also be found in the Bible, see 1 Corinthians 14:2, 23 (King James Version).

'Where the wilful weather-life wanders': this poem owes a debt to Francis Ponge's poem 'The End of Fall', translated by Robert Bly in *News of the Universe: Poems of Twofold Consciousness*, pp. 221–222.

www.ingramcontent.com/pod-product-compliance
Lightning Source LLC
Chambersburg PA
CBHW062156100526
44589CB00014B/1854